SUMMARY

SPARK

JOY

Marie Kondo

An Illustrated

Master Class on the Art of

Organizing and Tidying Up

Quick Summary

© **Copyright 2017 - Present. All rights reserved.**

This document is geared towards providing reliable information in regards to the topic and issue covered. The publication is sold with the idea that the publisher is not required to render accounting, officially permitted, or otherwise, qualified services. If advice is necessary, legal or professional, a practiced individual in the profession shall be ordered.

- From a Declaration of Principles which was accepted and approved equally by a Committee of the American Bar Association and a Committee of Publishers and Associations.

In no way is it legal to reproduce, duplicate, or transmit any part of this document in either electronic means or in printed format. Recording of this publication is strictly prohibited and any storage of this document is not allowed unless with written permission from the publisher. All rights reserved.

The information provided herein is stated to be truthful and consistent, in that any liability, in terms of inattention or otherwise, by any usage or abuse of any policies, processes, or directions contained within is solely and completely the responsibility of the recipient reader. Under no circumstances will any legal responsibility or blame be held against the publisher for any reparation, damages, or monetary loss due to the information herein, either directly or indirectly.

Respective authors own all copyrights not held by the publisher.

TABLE OF CONTENTS

INTRODUCTION 1

SUMMARY 2

    PART 1: CLEANING AND TIDYING 2

    PART 2: JOYFUL STORING 4

    PART 3: HOW TO PROPERLY TIDY CERTAIN ITEMS 5

    PART 4: TIDYING UP PAPERS 7

    PART 5: HOW TO TIDY UP KOMONO 8

    PART 6: SENTIMENTAL ITEMS AND TIDYING THE SPACE WE LIVE IN 10

    PART 7: WHY TIDY IN THE FIRST PLACE? 11

ANALYSIS 12

QUIZ 13

QUIZ ANSWERS 16

CONCLUSION 17

INTRODUCTION

Spark Joy is a book written by Marie Kondo. It is about organizing, tidying and how to properly organize an entire house. Some readers may ask themselves why we need a book about tidying and organizing the place where we live. But after reading this book, many readers will see that it is important how we organize the place where we sleep, eat and live.

Spark Joy is a manual and a guide for beginners for organizing a living space in the best way possible. The author's style of writing is fun, and reader-friendly. Readers will have the opportunity to learn some new ways to use the space where they live so it can be a lot more than just a space where they do daily chores. Kondo also uses many drawings to better illustrate what she wants to say, which adds more charm to an already interesting read.

Spark Joy is a book for everyone and anyone who wants their homes to spark with joy, and we will soon find out what makes the book so special.

SUMMARY

PART 1: CLEANING AND TIDYING

In the first part of the book, Kondo writes about tidying and cleaning and opens the book with a description of New Year's cleaning in Japan. The author says that in Japan it is normal to clean a house every year before the New Year; a similar custom exists in United States with "spring-cleaning".

After the short introduction, the author explains the difference between tidying and cleaning. She says that while cleaning usually means removing dirt, dust and other natural by-products of our everyday lives, tidying means something different. Tidying means to work on specific objects. This is the main difference between cleaning and tidying.

Now how do we properly tidy and organize the house?

To tidy a house it is vital to concentrate on discarding unneeded items. The first thing to do is to discard the unnecessary items, and later organize what remains. Discarding is not all a person should do, but the author suggests many people give up on this step.

The concept of tidying opens the way for some surprising and innovative ideas. That is why the author encourages her readers to try something new.

An error that many people make during the discard phase is that they keep a "box of maybes." Although some experts suggest a box of maybes could be useful, the author says that in reality this does not work well. Kondo provides her own example and says that when she decided to keep a box of maybes, every time she saw items in that box she felt guilty. She felt guilty because every time she passed the box and saw what was in it, she felt that she was discarding something she might need.

Often, after finishing the tidying and discarding phases, some do not feel satisfied. This often happens because the house lacks necessary color. The best way to keep a house colorful is to keep the house full of things we love. Emptiness brings dissatisfaction and even guilt, especially when we remember things that we discarded that were precious and dear to us.

PART 2: JOYFUL STORING

In this chapter the author writes about something she calls "joyful storing."

Storage should be temporary while tidying. Immediately when we begin tidying, our room will become messy. That is something natural, which is why the idea of storage in that phase is something temporary.

But is there a way to keep the maximum useful storage space?

According to Kondo there is.

One way to improve maximum usefulness of storage space is to place items made of the same material together. Put clothing with other clothing, while plastic belongs with other material made of plastic. The author also suggests paying attention to drawers and not allowing them to be more than 70% full because they will overflow.

Here the author mentions four of her main principles when it comes to storing items:

1. Items need to stand upright.
2. Items need to be stored in one spot.
3. Storage space should be divided into square compartments.
4. Items should be folded.

PART 3: HOW TO PROPERLY TIDY CERTAIN ITEMS

This chapter is about how to properly tidy clothes. As the author suggested earlier in her book, every tidying phase begins with tidying clothes. The first step towards successfully tidying clothes is to gather all clothes and put them in one place. It is important for all clothes to be in one place because after this, tidying can begin.

Kondo explains how to tidy clothes according to the different types of clothes that we have, like long-sleeved clothes, short-sleeved, camisoles, weird-shaped shirts, etc.

The clothes tidying process is followed by tidying books.

Tidying books may seem like an easy job, but when we take a closer look we will find out that it needs a lot more work than it may seem at first. According to the author, tidying books can increase our sensitivity to joy.

What makes people keep a book after they have already read it?

Well first, if a person reads a book and likes it, then there is a great possibility that they will keep it. According to the author, this means the book produced a "spark" and made the person keep it, rather than get rid of it immediately after reading it. Another reason people choose to keep their books is because of the sentimental value that a certain book has. Sentimental value is "born" when an item becomes especially precious and dear to us. Thus, that item becomes a memento. It reminds us of someone dear to us, so we keep it because it makes us feel close to them. Books are no different. Also, books are often precious gifts and mementos at the same time, because many people give books as presents to their beloved ones.

That is why books are to be tidied with special care and attention. When organizing books, it is important to keep two rules in mind: books should always be stored by category and they should always be stored standing up. The author suggests that we should never stack our books in one big pile.

When it comes to magazines or comic books, the situation is a bit different. A book has value, which is almost infinite, while a magazine has less value, especially if it is about something that is now considered outdated. Kondo suggests that we should decide on our own how many magazines we want to keep, but the number should be small and considered to be a "hall of fame."

PART 4: TIDYING UP PAPERS

When it comes to papers, we often think that one paper cannot make a mess. When it comes to just one, that is true. But what happens when we have dozens of documents and papers scattered around?

Before we decide which papers we want to throw away, the author suggests that we should gather all the documents and papers that we have into one place. After that we should divide them into individual sheets. Then we will decide which papers we need to discard and what to keep. When doing this the author says that we should make something that she calls the "pending box." A pending box is a small cardboard box, which will contain certain papers which need our attention immediately or a short period of time in the future. Papers which might be stored in a pending box are bills or letters which are to be sent off.

After doing this, we should also discard our credit card statements, but under the condition that we have paid our payment and that we rectified our balance. When this is done, the credit card statement has fulfilled its purpose and should be discarded to make some extra free space.

Warranties are different. Warranties are usually saved even after a long period of time has passed. The author suggests that we should store our warranties in one clear binder and that we should check the binder now and then for any expired warranty.

When it comes to papers like old instruction manuals, the author says that we should discard them. Manuals are rarely (if ever) read and they should be discarded. When it comes to items like greeting cards or postcards, we should keep them only if they "spark" joy within us. If they do not, and especially if they remind us of something unpleasant or that do not want to remember, we should definitely discard them.

PART 5: HOW TO TIDY UP KOMONO

Komono is the most difficult and the most complicated category to tidy, because Komono consists of things such as food supplies, electrical tools, stationery tools, cleaning supplies and much more. The author says that for each Komono category, there are three steps to successfully tidy them:

1. First, gather all items that belong to one category in one place.
2. The second is to choose only those items that spark joy.
3. The third step is to store the items by categories.

For example, when tidying up DVDs and CDs, the most important thing we should pay attention to is keeping only DVDs and CDs that spark joy. The rest of them we should consider junk and we should discard them as soon as possible. The situation is similar to books. We should keep CDs and DVDs that mean something to us in a way that they will produce joy within us. To be able to successfully do that, it is important for us not to listen to or watch the content of those CDs or DVDs.

When it comes to stationery supplies, they should be divided into three categories: paper-related supplies, letter-writing supplies, and equipment. Paper-related supplies are notebooks, diaries and similar items. We should discard any of these that has either fulfilled its purpose or no longer produces joy.

Under letter-writing supplies we put things like postcards, envelopes, letter papers and similar items.

When it comes to equipment we should discard anything that does not spark joy, especially items like pencils and pens.

Items that go under electrical Komono are batteries, memory cards, cords of all sorts, etc. Before we decide to discard something, we should check the purpose and use of the electrical Komono that is in our possession.

When it comes to skincare products and relaxing products, such as oils, candles, and aromatherapy products, the situation is the same: if they do not spark joy they should be discarded. When it comes to medication, we should also check the expiration date and if the medication has expired we should discard it.

PART 6: SENTIMENTAL ITEMS AND TIDYING THE SPACE WE LIVE IN

When tidying old items that often hold some sentimental value the situation is easy to solve. We should discard old items, such as uniforms, report cards and similar items. But the problem may occur when we tidy items that hold greater sentimental value like family photos. When dealing with these items we should carefully choose which items we want to keep and what we want to discard. For example, certain photos have greater value than others. Certain photos hold valuable memories for us and thus we should keep them.

When decorating entranceways, the author suggests that we should keep small things in order. When we talk about our living room, it is a room in which most of our free time will be spent and that is why it should be kept tidy. The kitchen should be kept clean, as well as being tidy. People who have home offices need to pay attention to the amount of unnecessary papers piling up. Every paper and document that is unneeded should be discarded.

In the bedroom, which should be everyone's place for ultimate rest and the place where we will refill our "battcries," we should keep it as clean as possible. Wash sheets and pillow cases regularly. The author suggests keeping bedroom light indirect and soft.

When it comes to bathrooms we should get rid of every unnecessary item, because our bathroom should have a natural and fresh aroma. Air fresheners are very useful, especially those with mild and pleasant aromas).

PART 7: WHY TIDY IN THE FIRST PLACE?

There is a big difference between a clean and tidy home and a messy one. When people return from work and see the place where they live is clean and tidy, it will bring them joy and satisfaction and they will feel less stressful.

A tidy place can influence how we feel and it can even help to regulate our stress level. Let's say that a person returns from work exhausted. The last thing this person needs is to tidy and clean the bathroom or bedroom. But if that person sees the place is already clean and there is no need for further cleaning, they will feel relaxed and will be able to rest after a long day of work.

When tidying and cleaning it is important to pay attention to what others mean and not to impose one person's opinion on them. Every person has their own way of performing tasks, so it's important not to force anyone to work one particular way. When tidying becomes part of our life, we can try to teach other people, by showing them how things can be done rather than force. That way, tidying will bring even more joy to our lives, and before we know it, the 'culture of tidying' will become a normal activity for many people.

ANALYSIS

The first time I opened this book, I expected that it would be a fiction novel about things that can "spark joy" in our lives. What I certainly did not expect was a book about cleaning and tidying. Yes, cleaning and tidying, because these two words have entirely different meanings. A person can clean a bathroom, but a bookshelf can be tidy. Anyway, even though the book is mostly about tidying and cleaning, surprisingly it is not some boring book of instructions for how to do this and how to do that. *Spark Joy* is actually a very interesting and educational book and readers will learn many things about how to properly tidy and clean (not tidy *or* clean but tidy *and* clean) everything around the house.

Let's admit: there are many of us who hate cleaning and tidying. Even if we don't hate it, we usually do it by quickly putting clothing items here and there; thinking that just because our clothes are not on the floor that everything is fine. Well, after reading *Spark Joy*, we will know how to tidy and clean everything there is, from old lightbulbs to that awful content of unknown origin that has been in the basement for ages. We will also learn there truly is joy that comes when we clean and tidy.

Marie Kondo's guidelines for cleaning and tidying are refreshing, interesting, reader-friendly and sparkling with joy.

Drawings inside the book show how things can be done, and I think it is good the book has some pictures in it. Without them, it would be just plain text, but with pictures we can visualize how to do what the author suggests, and that makes the whole thing much easier. A great book, definitely useful to have and even more useful to read, *Spark Joy* shows us how to find joy in chores that often don't seem joyful at all.

QUIZ

There is never enough knowledge, is there? That is why this quiz is written. Questions are simple and the answers are even simpler but for all readers who cannot find the answers in the summary section they are easy to find below in the "quiz answers" section.

Let's get started.

QUESTION 1

"In her first part of the book Kondo writes about tidying and cleaning and opens the book with a description of New Year's cleaning in North Korea."

                TRUE   FALSE

QUESTION 2

When we place items of the same material together that is called...?

    a) ...needful storing.
    b) ...joyful storing.
    c) ...playful storing.
    d) ...logical storing.

QUESTION 3

What 'kinds' of items are part of something the author calls as 'electrical Komono'?

a) Wires, cellphones, pipes, old toothbrushes.
b) Old coins, used computer keyboards, headphones.
c) Wires, part of car engine, cables.
d) Nothing above.

QUESTION 4

"The author says we should discard old instruction manuals. This is because manuals are rarely (if ever) read and they should be discarded."

         FALSE   TRUE

QUESTION 5

"_____ is what the author says the most difficult and the most complicated category to _____. This is because _____ consists of categories such as food supplies, electrical tools like cords, stationery tools, cleaning supplies and much more."

QUESTION 6

What is a 'box of maybes'?

   a) It is a box where we keep items that we do not want to discard.
   b) It is a box where we keep items that we are unsure whether to discard them or not.
   c) It is a box of items where we keep all the items that we will discard but not immediately.
   d) None of the above.

QUESTION 7

"A _____ is a small cardboard box, which will contain certain _____ which require our attention immediately or in shorter period of time in the future. _____, which can be stored in a _____, can be bills or letters, which are to be sent off."

QUESTION 8

"When tidying books it is very important to keep two things in mind: books should always be stored by color and they should always be stored the way that they should 'stand up.'"

                TRUE   FALSE

QUIZ ANSWERS

QUESTION 1 – FALSE

QUESTION 2 – b

QUESTION 3 – c

QUESTION 4 – TRUE

QUESTION 5 – "Komono, tidy, Komono."

QUESTION 6 – b

QUESTION 7 – "pending box, papers, papers, pending box."

QUESTION 8 – FALSE

CONCLUSION

I must confess that *Spark Joy* really sparked some joy in me, not only when I was reading the book, but also when I went through the process the author discusses.

I also must say that I have not seen many books that deal with tidying and cleaning in such a unique way. There are books in which authors talk and write about decorating our living space, with numerous tidbits of advice for how to make our living spaces more vibrant and lively. But there is something special about this book. It may be because the author broke the material she intended to talk about into several parts and then connected them back together into one meaningful whole. It may also be because there are many drawings and pictures, which are cute and "sparkly." I am not much of a tidying/cleaning literature reader, so this book was definitely something new for me. Personally, I thought that it was going to be some boring "do this and do that" book. I thought everything would revolve around trivial things such as where to place your favorite plant so your entire room gets the best ratio of light and shadow or similar stuff.

But I was wrong. *Spark Joy* is a book where everyone can learn at least one new thing about properly tidying and cleaning a bathroom, or what to do with those seven boxes of unknown papers. It is a book where almost everyone will find something that they will be able to apply in their own household.

The book also has drawings to illustrate the author's points. Drawings, pictures and visualization are vital for many people, especially when it comes to business that includes scheduling items in a specific order. Some readers may not like this book, but that is up for everyone to decide for themselves. But whoever reads it will have the opportunity to learn something new which can be applied immediately to improve their surroundings.

And I suggest that all readers of this summary read the book because the author presents us with the knowledge we need to make the places we live even more comfortable and "livable."

Spark Joy will surely spark some joy, not only while reading it but also when the reader realizes that tidying and cleaning can be something more than just taking care of chores.

Thank You, and more…

Thank you for spending your time to read this book, I hope now you hold a greater knowledge about **Spark Joy.**

There are like-minded individuals like you who would like to learn about **Spark Joy,** this information can be useful for them as well. So, I would highly appreciate if you post a good review on amazon kindle where you purchased this book. And to share it in your social media (Facebook, Instagram, etc.)

Not only does it help me make a living, but it helps others obtain this knowledge as well. So I would highly appreciate it!!

www.amazon.com

We have other summary books available for you as well.

1- Summary - The Code of Extraordinary Mind:
https://www.amazon.com/dp/B071JCNZCN/

2- Summary - Commonwealth:
https://www.amazon.com//dp/B0731M6432/

3- Summary- The Undoing Project
https://www.amazon.com/dp/B071G8BRFK/

4- Summary - 13 Things Mentally Strong People Don't Do

https://www.amazon.com/dp/B0719S6PPN/

5- Summary - Drive: By Daniel Pink - The Surprising Truth About What Motivates Us
https://www.amazon.com/dp/B0727MQR4Z/

Thank you for taking the time to read this book, please give us a good review on Amazon to support us, so we (my team and I) can make more summaries for you!

---

https://www.amazon.com/s/ref=nb_sb_noss?url=search-alias=aps&field-keywords=quicksummary&rh=i%3Aaps,k%3Aquicksummary

Feel free to follow us on social media to get notified of future summaries.

1- *Facebook: BookSummaries*
https://www.facebook.com/BookSummaries-1060732983986564/

2- *Instagram: BookSummaries*
https://www.instagram.com/booksummaries/

Made in the USA
Lexington, KY
16 January 2019